HOW FAR CAN YOU GO WITH
Twenty-Five Cents?

Written by: Janet Wright-Moore
Illustrated by: Sherman Beck

ISBN: 978-0-692-94718-0

For "Jabby" and "P'nut"
Always remember and never forget....
YOU come from greatness!

How far can you go with twenty-five cents?

Twenty-five cents is one quarter: twenty-five pennies! It's not much money at all. Well...it's not much money to most but, to Grandpop, it was!

He worked and he strived
With a twinkle in his eye
He worked hard to show
Just how far you can go!

Grandpop's father sent him to college with just twenty-five cents!

Twenty-five cents wasn't much money, but it was going to take Grandpop far. It would take him away from the tobacco farm and away from being poor.

Twenty-five cents was going to pay for his college education!

Grandpop bid his father goodbye and set out on his long journey to college.

He walked and he thought and he thought as he walked...

I'll work and I'll strive
With a twinkle in my eye
I'll work hard to show
Just how far I can go!

Days later, Grandpop made it to the college campus. He could hardly contain his excitement as he entered the office to sign up for classes.

"I am here to attend college!"
he proudly announced and placed
his quarter on the counter.

"Twenty-five cents?" the men laughed
as they asked...

*How far can you go with
twenty-five cents?*

"What's so funny?" he thought,
but soon found out why
they were laughing.

College cost much, much more
than twenty-five cents.

Grandpop didn't have enough money!
He would have to work,
and work,
and work

before he could start college.

Grandpop didn't want to go back home.

He thought about how hard his father worked to give him money for college.

He thought about how far he could go in life with a college education.

He decided to leave his twenty-five cents as the down payment for classes.

He worked and he strived
With a twinkle in his eye
He worked hard to show
Just how far you can go!

That first year was hard for Grandpop as he watched the students go to their classes.

He wanted to go to school with them, but he worked and saved his money thinking...

10

I'll work and I'll strive
With a twinkle in my eye
I'll work hard to show
Just how far I can go!

After Grandpop worked a whole year, he went back to that office and proudly placed all the money he made on the counter.

That's when he learned it would only pay for one year of classes.

He worked and he strived
With a twinkle in his eye
He worked hard to show
Just how far you can go!

Determined to go far, Grandpop left the money at the office and went to classes that year.

The next year he didn't go to classes, but worked and saved his money.

He would work a year, save his money, and then go to classes a year.

Work a year, save his money,
go to classes.

Work a year, save his money,
go to classes.

Work a year, save his money,
go to classes.

Grandpop did this for eight years!

Finally, eight years later, after leaving home with just twenty-five cents, Grandpop graduated from college!

He worked and he strived
With a twinkle in his eye
He worked hard to show
Just how far you can go!

Grandpop would go on to marry, have children, become a pastor and receive three other college degrees.

A college even holds a special honor in his name.

So the next time you hold twenty-five cents
in your hand, or feel like you can't
do whatever you believe you can do...

22

Remember...

If you work and you strive
With a twinkle in your eye
You will work hard to show
Just how far you can go!

CPSIA information can be obtained
at www.ICGtesting.com
Printed in the USA
BVHW020032020522
635871BV00034B/1131

9 780692 947180